YUMMY
IT'S ALL ABOUT BALANCE

DANNI DUNCAN

Copyright @ Danielle Duncan
Published by Ingram
Photography by Michelle Bolitho
Design by Helena Berggren

ISBN: 978-0-6454738-0-3
Hardback Edition

All rights reserved. The moral right of the author has been asserted. No part of this book may be reproduced in any mechanical, photographic or electronic process; nor may it be stored in a retrieval system, transmitted or otherwise be copied for public or private use, without written permission from the author. You must not circulate this book in any format.
This publication contains the opinions and ideas of the author. It is intended to provide helpful and informative material on the subjects addressed. While the author has used their best efforts in preparing this publication, the material is of the nature of general comment only. Any use of information in this book is at the reader's discretion and risk. The author can not be held responsible for any loss, claim or damage arising out of the use, or misuse, of any suggestions made, or for any material on third party websites.

CONTENTS

ABOUT YUMMY	1
ABOUT FOOD	3
ABOUT BALANCE	11
BREAKFASTS	19
PASTAS AND SALADS	35
MAINS	53
SIDES	77
TREATS AND SMOOTHIES	95
HOW TO COOK	102
THANK YOU	111
ABOUT THE AUTHOR	112
FURTHER READING	124
INDEX	125

KEYS

TREATS = Enjoy these foods from time to time.

LEAN & CLEAN = Every day foods that are delicious and full of great nutrients.

HEY THERE!

Thanks for bringing Yummy to your home.

Firstly, I am so excited that you've grabbed my book. As a certified nutrition coach, fitness trainer, Master Female Trainer and mum I am so passionate about educating people in living a balanced, healthy life – without cutting out food, incorporating restrictive diets and excluding yourself from social situations.

Life is about living and a huge part of that is eating. Eating whole, nutritious food whilst indulging in treats and things that fill your soul. I am a true believer that you don't have to cut out your favourites to hit your goals. It's all about balance and knowing what your body needs.

This book encompasses all that I love about food and health. From high protein dishes, clean salads, hearty pastas, nutrient dense and high protein snacks to quick sides and some good old recipes from my Nana who is all about the sweet treats. Nana definitely wasn't worried about macros - and there's nothing better than a cup of tea with her Caramel Slice or Cookies.

I've popped a key in here as well, so you know whether it's something you could have on the daily - or something you would savour as a treat, here and there. Remember it's all about balance and serving size. Allowing yourself to have a treat from time to time will stop you from bingeing and going crazy - and knowing that you are fuelling your body with good, nutritious food means you're giving yourself the best opportunity to reach your goals.

xo Danni

WE EAT FOR 4 REASONS: HEALTH, NUTRITION, ENJOYMENT AND SOCIALISATION.

those last two are just as important as the first two.

ABOUT FOOD

There are a few things you need to know if you are on a fitness, health or fat loss journey - and that's what your food is doing for you. There are 3 Macronutrients: (Well there are 4 but we don't talk about Alcohol as an energy source... but everyone knows, I love a cheeky wine.)

- Protein
- Carbohydrate
- Fats

Knowing how these fuel you and what falls into each category can help you to achieve your goals.

PROTEIN

Protein is essential for muscle repair and muscle growth. It is also the building blocks of our bones, cartilage, skin, blood and is essential for fat loss.

Ensuring you have enough lean protein sources throughout the day means you are more likely to hit your goals. The average adult needs 0.8g/kg of body weight to sustain normal life (sedentary) and up to 2g/kg body weight if you're wanting to build muscle. There are 4 calories per gram of protein. Protein sources include animal and non animal proteins.

Some good protein sources include:

CHICKEN (breast/tenderloin)	**TUNA**	**WHITE FISH**	**SALMON**

RED MEAT (beef/lamb/pork)	**SEEDS**	**ASPARGUS**	**SPINACH**

EGGS	**BROCCOLI**	**SHELLFISH**	**DAIRY** (cheese/yoghurt/milk)

NUTS	**LEGUMES**	**OATS**	**QUINOA**

CARBOHYDRATES

Carbohydrates are our main energy source. We need carbohydrates, and cutting them out does more than just restrict your energy. Carbohydrates fuel your nervous system, your working muscles and are important for brain function and your metabolism.

The thing to remember with carbs is that they're not all created equal. Carbohydrates are categorised by a scale called Glycemic Index (GI), a number between 1-100 according to how much they increase your blood sugar. Ensuring 80% of your carbohydrate intake is made up of **LOW GI** carbohydrate is important - as diets with a high GI have been linked to diabetes and obesity. There are 4 calories per gram of carbohydrate.

Low GI foods (0-55) are usually whole grain products such as:

SOUR DOUGH BREAD	**FRUITS**	**SOY PRODUCTS**	**ROLLED OATS**

QUINOA	**VEGETABLES**	**SWEET POTATO**	**LEGUMES**

MULTIGRAIN BREAD	**BROWN RICE**	**PASTA**	**WHOLE GRAINS**

High GI foods (70 plus) are usually refined grains and those with added sugar, such as:

- White Potatoes
- White Bread
- White Rice
- Lollies
- Cereals
- White Wraps
- Sandwich Thins
- Prepackaged Food

FATS

Good fats - monounsaturated and polyunsaturated - are great for the heart, cholesterol and lower the risk of heart disease and stroke. Fat also helps support cell growth, helps your body to keep warm and supports organ function. **You need good fats.**

There are 9 calories per gram of fat - hence why our body doesn't need as many. Fats should be consumed in moderation with the understanding that calories can easily add up when you're consuming fats.

As an energy source fats are great for long term and endurance activities. Fats are harder to turn into an energy source than carbohydrate as they require more oxygen to do this. However it is essential for high intensity exercise as your body requires fat to access stored carbohydrates. If the body consumes too much fat however - that can't turn into energy - it is then stored.

Some good fats sources are:

AVOCADO

OILY FISH
(salmon)

CACAO

OLIVE OIL

NUTS

EGGS

SEEDS

CHEESE

MICRO-NUTRIENTS

Micronutrients are all of the vitamins and minerals your body needs. They are necessary for your immune system, energy production, bone health and ensuring that your organs function properly.

ENSURING YOU HAVE A BALANCED, COLOURFUL DIET MEANS YOU ARE MORE LIKELY TO GET ALL OF YOUR REQUIRED MICRONUTRIENTS.

ABOUT BALANCE

WHY I EAT THIS WAY

For years in my early 20's I restricted myself - wanting to be lean and strong, but not really realising that not only did I need to eat in order to do this, but I was also missing out on the social aspect of good food.

Into my mid to late 20's I started eating better; enjoying food in social situations as well as at home. I started moving my body better and found a balance. Not only was I achieving my goals and able to push myself further, but all aspects of my life improved. I had more clarity, I had more patience, I was more productive, I slept better and had more energy on a daily basis. I was able to overcome adversity more easily. I enjoyed socialising with friends and family and never restricted myself. I could enjoy a wine, some chocolate, cake, dinners out and not interrupt my goals.

When I fell pregnant with Harper and entered motherhood food fueled me and helped me in so many ways. Ensuring my body could grow a human, produce milk and then recover and rebuild postpartum. I eagerly studied to achieve my Nutrition Coach certification so I could help other women achieve their goals without restriction. Eating for health, eating for nutrition, eating for enjoyment and eating for socialisation. Know that you don't have to be perfect every day - one hot day doesn't make a Summer, and knowing what is required to continue working towards your goals is a huge step!

I hope this book provides you with inspiration to live a balanced, healthy lifestyle just like me.

WATER

Water is essential to living. Not only does our body need water to aid in digestion and gut health, absorb nutrients, provide us with energy and regulate our body temperature - but it is hugely important for our brain function. Without it, your concentration will wander, your brain will feel foggy and you will feel tired. In general, adults need to drink a minimum of 3% of their body weight if they are sedentary.

SO, DRINK UP!

FAMILY EATING

What I love about my recipes is that they are all family friendly. Harper loves all of these meals and for me it's important that we can eat as a family. Getting kids involved in cooking is a great way to educate them around the importance of good food and sets up good relationships with food from early on.

EXERCISE AND MOVING YOUR BODY

As part of a healthy, balanced lifestyle, moving your body is hugely important. Health.gov.au recommends that adults should be active most days. Each week adults should do between 2.5 to 5 hours of moderate intensity physical activity such as a brisk walk and 1.25 to 2.5 hours of vigorous intensity physical activity, or a combination of the 2.

Moving your body not only contributes to your energy expenditure during the day (therefore increasing the amount of food you can consume), but assists in increasing your bone density, is essential for strong joints and increases your metabolism. Exercise also releases endorphins which in turn makes you feel happier, more productive, more patient and gives you a sense of accomplishment.

"MOVING YOUR BODY NOT ONLY CONTRIBUTES TO YOUR ENERGY EXPENDITURE DURING THE DAY BUT ASSISTS IN INCREASING YOUR BONE DENSITY"

So now that you know my why -
I hope you enjoy every single one of my recipes and I inspire you to look after your health, not only for now, but for the future too. Good luck and happy cooking!

LOVE & LIFE

xo Danni

"Let food be thy food and medicine"

"...y medicine be thy food"

— HIPPOCRATES

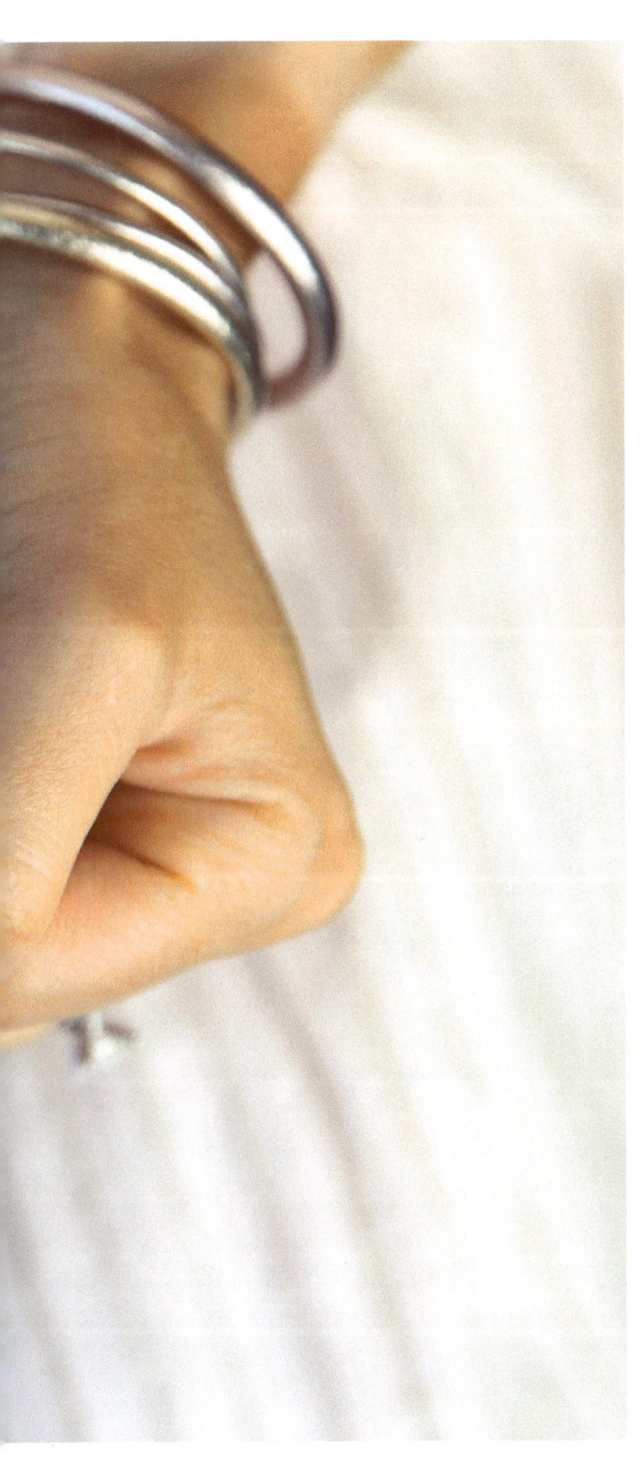

BREAKFASTS

My absolute favourite meal of the day. Sweet or savoury, hot or cold, there are so many options. I wake up so excited for breakfast each and every day. There's no better way to kickstart the day with a good nutritious, yummy breaky.

BREAKFAST ◊ TREATS

CREPES

My mum used to make these when we were kids and we'd help. It was so fun lining up the lemon wedges and the sugar bowl and rolling them up to gobble down. We never waited until they were all done - we'd eat as she cooked.

MAKES: 6 (2 serves)	KCAL/SERVE: 380 *(without toppings)*	C: 54g P: 15g F: 9g

INGREDIENTS

- 1 egg
- 1 Tbsp sugar
- 1 cup flour
- 1.5 cups milk

METHOD

1. Beat egg and sugar. Add flour and milk and mix well.

2. Spray a medium fry pan with olive oil over medium heat.

3. Add enough batter to thinly coat the base, and tilt the pan to create an even thickness. It should take just a minute before the edge curls and the base turns golden.

4. Flip and cook for a further minute. Add your toppings then roll them up and serve hot.

Toppings: lemon and sugar, banana, strawberries, other berries, maple syrup - *whatever tickles your fancy.*

BREAKFAST ◊ LEAN & CLEAN

BANANA PANCAKES

I started making pancakes like this when Harper was 6 months old - and realised how delicious they were. They are great for the whole family for breaky or make in advance for a fab snack on the go.

SERVES: 1	KCAL/SERVE: 294 *(without toppings)*	C: 52g P: 17g F: 8g

INGREDIENTS

- 1 banana
- 1 egg
- 15g oats
- 1 tsp chia seeds
- 10g vanilla protein powder
- 1/2 tsp cinnamon
- 1/2 tsp vanilla extract

Toppings
- Berries
- 80g yoghurt (flavour of your choice)
- 15ml maple syrup

METHOD

1. Mash banana then beat in the egg.
2. Stir in oats, chia seeds, vanilla protein powder, cinnamon and vanilla extract.
3. Pour mixture onto a fry pan and into circles with a 5cm diameter.
4. Cook for 3 minute each side or until cooked.
5. Add berries, yoghurt and 15ml maple syrup to serve.

Hint: these are fabulous for the kids too!

GRANOLA

Nothing better than a crunchy granola with some yoghurt & fruit - the supermarket ones just don't hit the spot for me. This is so yummy for breaky or sprinkle on some yoghurt for a quick snack.

SERVES: 10

KCAL/SERVE: 247 (50g)

C: 32g P: 6g F: 10.6g

INGREDIENTS

- 2.5 cups rolled oats
- 1/4 cup shredded coconut
- 1/4 cup sultanas
- 6 pitted dates, roughly chopped
- 1/4 cup cranberries
- 1/4 cup slivered almonds
- 1/4 cup chia seeds
- 1/2 cup crushed walnuts
- 1 Tbsp melted coconut oil
- 30ml honey
- 60ml maple syrup

RHUBARB P. 107

--- **BREAKFAST ◊ LEAN & CLEAN** ---

METHOD

1. Mix all ingredients except the honey and maple syrup.

2. Pour on a baking tray lined with baking paper and place in a 150 degree oven for 15 minutes.

3. Remove and drizzle honey over the mixture and mix. Place back in the oven for 10 minutes.

4. Remove and drizzle maple syrup over the mixture and mix again for an even coating. Place back in the oven for 10 minutes, watching that it doesn't start to burn.

5. Remove and leave to cool - this is when it'll start to crisp up.
   Once cool, put it in an airtight container.

Note: Serve with poached pears, rhubarb, or your favourite yoghurt and fruit.

BREAKFAST ◊ LEAN & CLEAN

OVERNIGHT OATS

*Like a chocolate smoothie bowl but with so much goodness.
No need to worry about cooking breaky as this is ready to go in the fridge,
ready for the next day and is bloody delicious.*

SERVES: 3	KCAL/SERVE: 264	C: 39g P: 15g F: 6g

INGREDIENTS

- 120 grams rolled oats
- 1 banana
- 1 scoop chocolate whey protein powder
- 1 tsp cacao powder
- 250ml unsweetened almond milk
- your favourite berries
- hazelnuts
- shaved coconut

METHOD

1. Put 40 grams of oats in each container.

2. In a blender or Nutribullet put banana, protein powder, cacao powder and almond milk and blend well.

3. Pour mixture over the oats, making sure they are well covered.

4. Top with your favourite berries, hazelnuts and shaved coconut and leave in the fridge overnight.

5. *Voilá - delicious!*

POACHED PEARS P. 106

BREAKFAST ◊ LEAN & CLEAN

PORRIDGE

I don't know how many times I've heard people say they don't like porridge - then try this recipe and their lives change forever. No watery gruel here, creamy goodness only! (Don't forget the poached pears.)

SERVES: 1	KCAL/SERVE: 366	C: 61g P: 7g F: 7g

INGREDIENTS

- 35g rolled oats
- 190ml unsweetened almond milk
- 1 banana, sliced
- 1/2 tsp cinnamon
- 1/2 tsp vanilla extract
- 1 tsp whole flaxseeds
- 15ml honey

METHOD

1. Put all ingredients, except the honey over a medium heat and slowly cook, continuing to stir until nice and creamy.

2. Serve with honey, rhubarb or poached pears.

   (If you want to increase your protein, add 10g of your favourite protein powder during cooking.)

EGGS 4 WAYS

SCRAMBLED

Mix 2 eggs in a bowl with salt, pepper and some chopped chives.

Heat a small fry pan to low - medium heat. (Spray with olive oil or pop 5g of butter for a more creamy indulgent scramble.) Pour in the mixture and continue folding with a spatula until cooked.

Serve on hot sourdough and enjoy.

POACHED

Break your eggs carefully into a petri dish each.

Bring a pot of water half filled to a gentle simmer and add a tablespoon of white vinegar. Make a whirlpool with a knife and slowly pour in the eggs one at a time. (I wouldn't do more than 2 at a time.)

Simmer for 3 minutes for soft poached eggs. Gently remove with a slotted spoon.

Serve on sourdough with a side of spinach and cherry tomatoes with a drizzle of balsamic vinegar.

BOILED

Bring a pot of water to the boil with 1 Tbsp of white vinegar. Lower room temperature eggs in slowly. Cook for 5 minutes for soft boiled or 10 minutes for hard boiled.

Crack off the top, season and enjoy with toasted sourdough soldiers.

OMELETTE

- 2 eggs
- 1 mushroom
- 3 cherry tomatoes
- handful of baby spinach
- 10g colby cheese
- 50g smoked salmon (optional)
- chives

Mix 2 eggs in a bowl with a diced mushroom, chopped cherry tomatoes, small handful of chopped baby spinach, salmon, salt and pepper.

Pour into a medium hot pan sprayed with olive oil. Let it cook, every now and then lifting the edges to let more egg mixture under the omelette.

Sprinkle with cheese, fold over the omelette.

Serve with toasted sourdough and fresh chives.

PASTAS AND SALADS

Pasta is a fabulous source of carbohydrates and long lasting energy. Remember it is more dense than other carbohydrates so I suggest enjoying pasta once, no more than twice a week. This is why I have put it as both *'Treats'* as well as *'Lean and Clean'*. There are loads of nutrients in all of my pasta dishes, so never fear, they are fuelling your body.

These salads can be made as a meal or used as a side to your favourite protein. Great for entertaining, for the whole family or to meal prep for your weekly lunches.

PASTAS & SALADS

CHICKEN AND BACON CARBONARA

Is there a better pasta on a cold day than a creamy carbonara? An all time favourite, this is just as delicious without the heaviness of cream.

SERVES: 3	KCAL/SERVE: 555	C: 53g P: 42g F: 12g

TREATS ◊ LEAN & CLEAN

INGREDIENTS

- 1 Tbsp coconut oil
- 100g smoked back bacon, chopped in to 1cm strips
- 3 spring onions, chopped
- 1 chilli, chopped finely
- 2 garlic cloves, chopped finely
- 100g mushrooms, sliced
- 300g skinless chicken breast, chopped in to 1cm strips
- 200g spaghetti
- 2 egg yolks
- 1 tsp dijon mustard
- juice of 1 lemon
- 8 cherry tomatoes, halved

METHOD

1. Heat the oil in a pan and add the bacon, spring onions, chilli, garlic and mushrooms. Cook for about 2 minutes.

2. Add the chicken and cook for about 6 minutes - or until cooked through. Add the cherry tomatoes.

3. Bring a pot of water to the boil and add the spaghetti.

4. While that's cooking; whisk the egg yolks, mustard and lemon juice and before you drain the pasta add 4 tablespoons of the starchy water from the pasta to the egg mixture and whisk well.

5. Drain the pasta and add it to the chicken mixture, season with salt and pepper and add the egg mixture. Stir to combine on a medium heat.

6. Serve with some parmesan cheese and a side salad. *Enjoy!*

SALMON AND BROCCOLI PASTA

Need a quick dinner that everyone will love? This is it! This came about when I literally only had salmon and broccoli in the fridge and it only takes 20 minutes.

SERVES: 4	KCAL/SERVE: 541	C: 57g P: 23g F: 19g

INGREDIENTS

- 3 x 110g salmon fillets
- 385g linguine (Or any pasta to be honest, I love fresh pasta but dried is fine.)
- 250ml Philadelphia Cream for Cooking light (this can be substituted with light sour cream if you can't find this brand)
- 200g broccoli (cut into small florets)
- 1 lemon, juiced and rind
- 2 cloves of garlic, crushed
- 3 spring onions, sliced
- handful of fresh dill, chopped finely
- 1/2 Tbsp extra virgin olive oil

METHOD

1. Put the salmon on a baking tray and season with salt and pepper. Pop it in a 180 degree oven for 15 minutes.

2. Heat the oil in a pan and add the garlic, onion and lemon rind. Stir until fragrant (about 2 minutes).

3. Add the cream, lemon juice and dill. Then add the salmon – breaking it up as you put it in. Season well.

4. Cook the pasta as per instructions then add the broccoli for the last 3 minutes (fresh pasta will only take 3 minutes so put it all in together). Drain and keep 2 Tbsp of the pasta water. Add the Broccoli and pasta to the sauce with the leftover water and a decent amount of sea salt. Mix together and serve.

PASTAS & SALADS

CHICKEN AND SUNDRIED TOMATO PASTA

This is Chris' favourite pasta dish! I make this most Friday nights before his Saturday football. Great energy source and creamy deliciousness.

SERVES: 4	**KCAL/SERVE:** 623	**C:** 72g **P:** 38g **F:** 18g

INGREDIENTS

- 400g fresh pasta - I like spirals or rigatoni. (If you can't get fresh - dried is fine.)
- 1 brown onion, diced
- 1 clove garlic, finely chopped or crushed
- 5ml extra virgin olive oil
- 400g chicken breast or tenderloins, diced small pieces
- 125g sun-dried tomatoes, chopped
- 1 cup mushrooms, sliced
- 400ml passata
- 250g Philadelphia Cream for Cooking light (this can be substituted with light sour cream if you can't find this brand)

METHOD

1. Cook pasta as per instructions on the packet.
2. Heat olive oil in the pan and fry onion and garlic until soft.
3. Season chicken with salt and pepper - add to the pan. Cook until browned.
4. Add sun-dried tomatoes and mushrooms for 3 minutes.
5. Add the passata then cook for about 5 minutes. Season well.
6. Drain the pasta and transfer it to the chicken mixture.
7. Turn off the heat and stir in the cream for cooking until all combined.
8. Serve with parmesan. *Voila!*

PASTAS & SALADS

PRAWN AND CHORIZO PASTA WITH GARLIC AND CHILLI

I mean, do I need to explain why this is so good? Prawn and Chorizo Pasta with Garlic and Chilli has to be one of my all time favourite pasta dishes. With a cold glass of Rose, is there anything better?

SERVES: 4	**KCAL/SERVE:** 566	**C:** 52g **P:** 27g **F:** 27g

INGREDIENTS

- 400g spaghetti (fresh if possible)
- 240g chorizo (or 2 links) sliced
- 15ml extra virgin olive oil
- 10g butter
- 4 cloves of garlic, finely sliced
- 1 birdseye chilli (I remove the seeds and finely slice.)
- 1 red chilli, finely sliced
- 300g prawns (I used frozen cooked ones but you can get fresh raw or cooked if you like. Raw will need a little more time to cook)
- 1/4 cup white wine
- 8 cherry tomatoes, halved
- 1/2 cup fresh parsley, chopped
- Parmesan to serve

METHOD

1. Cook the spaghetti as per instructions.
2. Fry off the chorizo (no oil needed) until cooked – set aside.
3. Add the oil & butter to a pan – add the garlic and chilli and cook until fragrant.
4. Add the prawns and wine then cook for 3 minutes.
5. Add the cherry tomatoes, parsley and chorizo. Cook until the prawns are cooked – they won't take long.
6. Stir through the spaghetti and serve with parmesan. *Voila! Delish!*

PASTAS & SALADS ◊ LEAN & CLEAN

PUMPKIN, BEETROOT AND GOATS CHEESE SALAD

A crowd pleaser. This one is great for a BBQ or dinner with friends - match it with lamb cutlets, a roast, or your favourite pie.

SERVES: 4

KCAL/SERVE: 376

C: 20g **P:** 10.2g **F:** 28g

INGREDIENTS

- 75g baby spinach
- 4 spring onions, finely sliced
- 125g baby beetroot halved
- 6 cherry tomatoes halved
- 200g avocado, diced
- 400g pumpkin
- 80g goats cheese
- 50g pine nuts (Lightly toasted on a fry pan for 3 minutes.)
- balsamic vinegar

METHOD

1. Chop the pumpkin into cubes, cover with 5ml of olive oil and a sprinkle nutmeg and pop in a 200 degree oven for 20 minutes.

2. Pop all ingredients in a bowl and dress with balsamic vinegar. Voilá!

SALMON P. 104

PASTAS & SALADS ◊ LEAN & CLEAN

GRAIN SALAD

This almost needs a disclaimer because you will totally be reaching for seconds! A great dish to prepare for lunches or as an addition to a family dinner.

SERVES: 6	KCAL/SERVE: 354	C: 49g P: 12g F: 13g

INGREDIENTS

- 1 cup quinoa
- 1/2 cup puy lentils
- 1/4 cup freekeh
- 8 cherry tomatoes, diced
- 1 bunch coriander, chopped
- 1/2 bunch flat leaf parsley, chopped
- 1/2 red onion, chopped finely
- 2 Tbsp toasted pumpkin seeds
- 2 Tbsp toasted slivered almonds
- 2 Tbsp toasted pine nuts
- 2 Tbsp baby capers
- 1/2 cup currants
- 1 pomegranate
- juice of 1 lemon
- 3 Tbsp olive oil
- salt and pepper

Best served with a piece of baked salmon (not included in the calories).

METHOD

1. Cook the quinoa, freekeh and lentils as per below.

2. Place quinoa in a pot and cover with an inch of water. Bring to the boil then turn on low and put the lid on. Cook for 10-15 minutes or until water has absorbed. Fluff with a fork and set aside.

3. Place the lentils and freekeh in a pot and cover with an inch of water. Bring to the boil, then reduce heat and cook for 20 minutes or until lentils and freekeh start to soften. Drain and set aside.

4. Place all other ingredients in a large bowl - add quinoa, freekeh and lentils. Add lemon juice, olive oil and season well. Top with dressing.

Dressing

- 1/2 cup Greek yoghurt
- 1 tsp cumin
- 1 Tbsp honey

— PASTAS & SALADS —

BROCCOLI AND KALE SALAD

*Another great one for a BBQ or family dinner,
lots of flavours and textures make it fresh and delicious.*

SERVES: 4	**KCAL/SERVE:** 235	**C:** 20g **P:** 7g **F:** 16g

INGREDIENTS

- 3 cups of broccoli
- 70 grams of kale
- 6 baby beetroot
- 30 grams of currants
- 50 grams of walnuts. chopped
- 25 grams of sunflower seeds
- 15 cherry tomatoes, halved
- 3 spring onions, chopped

Dressing

- 2 tsp extra virgin olive oil
- 30ml red wine vinegar
- 1 tsp dijon mustard
- 1 clove of garlic
- salt and pepper to taste

METHOD

1. Steam the broccoli florets until just cooked.

2. Massage the kale with a drop of olive oil to soften.

3. Toast the walnuts and the sunflower seeds in a pan until golden.

4. Pop it all into a bowl and pour over the dressing.

   Delicious with either a salmon fillet or lamb cutlets.

MAINS

Main meals don't have to be fancy or take you hours. I'm all about easy meals that the whole family love. Most of these can be frozen too and are great for leftovers the next day for lunch or dinner. Pair them with a salad or some steamed veggies or have them as they are.

BROTH P. 103

CHICKEN AND VEGETABLE SOUP

This recipe almost didn't make it in. I thought, who wants a soup recipe? Turns out, everyone! So here it is. If you can't make your own broth, you can use a store bought one.

SERVES: 8	KCAL/SERVE: 348	C: 37g P: 25g F: 9g

INGREDIENTS

- 2 Litres chicken broth (see broth recipe)
- Chicken from a whole roast chicken
- 375g soup mix (if you can't get soup mix you can use a combination of pearl barley, peas, lentils & beans)
- 250g sweet potato, diced in small cubes
- 250g potato, diced in small cubes
- 1 carrot, diced
- 50g frozen peas

METHOD

1. Make up the broth then add stripped chicken, soup mix, potatoes and carrot. Simmer, covered, over a low heat for 2 hours. Stir intermittently.

2. Season well and enjoy.

3. Serve with warm crusty bread - sourdough is my favourite.

TACO BOWLS

Mexican is a favourite in this house and taco bowls are super fun.

SERVES: 3	KCAL/SERVE: 294 bowl (+150 if adding brown rice)	C: 16g P: 37g F: 22g

INGREDIENTS

- 1 red onion, diced
- 1 clove of garlic, crushed
- 4 mushrooms, diced
- 1 capsicum, diced
- 500g lean beef mince
  (Or 500g turkey mince.)
- coriander
- 1 avocado
- 1 lime
- 200g cherry tomatoes

- iceberg lettuce, shredded
- carrot, grated
- light sour cream
- tomato salsa
- taco shells or Mission tortilla strips
- 400g tin of red kidney beans
- Taco Spice mix *(recipe on the next page)*

(Optional - 250g cooked brown rice, not included in the calories)

MAINS ◊ LEAN & CLEAN

INGREDIENTS - SPICE MIX

- 1 tsp garlic powder
- 1 tsp onion powder
- 1 tsp dried oregano
- 2 tsp cumin
- 2 tsp paprika
- ¼ tsp chilli powder (optional)
- 1 tsp salt

(Or just grab 1 packet of Taco Spice Mix)

BOWL 1

1. Smash the avocado with a fork.
2. Add salt and pepper.
3. Add 1/3 of the coriander.
4. Squeeze of lime.

BOWL 2

1. Chop the tomatoes in quarters.
2. Add 1/2 the onion.
3. Add 1/3 of the coriander roughly chopped.
4. Salt and pepper.

METHOD

1. Cook 1/2 the onion, garlic, mushrooms and capsicum for 3 minutes.
2. Add the mince and cook until brown.
3. Add the taco mix with 1/2 cup of water, 1/3 of the coriander and the beans. Season well.
4. Bring to the boil then turn down to low and leave to simmer.

TO ASSEMBLE

1. Put the lettuce in the bottom of a large bowl. (Pop the rice here too if adding.)
2. Add the mince, tomato mix, avocado mix, grated carrot, sour cream and salsa on top.
3. Break up the taco shells and crumble on top.
4. VOILA! Mix it all together and eat away.

Tip: If you already have some kangaroo chilli mix done, save time and use this instead.

MAINS ◊ LEAN & CLEAN

CHICKEN STIR FRY

Such an easy, nutritious meal that covers all bases - carbs, veggies and your dose of protein. I've put chicken here as it's a firm favourite but you can substitute with 300g of diced tofu if you want to make it vegetarian.

SERVES: 4	KCAL/SERVE: 296	C: 27g P: 34g F: 4g

INGREDIENTS

- 400g chicken tenderloins (or 300g Tofu diced into 1cm pieces)
- 2 large carrots, sliced into circles
- 1 cup of broccoli chopped into florets
- 8 mushrooms, sliced
- 150g snow peas
- 1 tin baby corn
- 1 capsicum
- 1 brown onion, sliced
- 4 cloves garlic, crushed or finely sliced
- 2cm piece of ginger
- 1/4 cup Sweet soy sauce (kecap manis)
- 3ml sesame oil
- 1 Tbsp honey
- 1/4 cup oyster sauce

METHOD

1. Pan fry the chicken and set aside.

2. Heat a wok and add all of the vegetables, ginger and garlic. Mix for 1 minute until combined then add 2 Tbsp of water. Continue stirring for another 2 minutes then cover for 2 minutes.

3. Remove the lid and add chicken back in and add the sauces. Continue cooking for another 3 minutes until all combined and veggies are cooked.

4. If you want to, you can add noodles or rice. (I use Fantastic instant noodles or brown rice.)

5. Soften 2 cakes of noodles then add to the stir fry when you add the chicken and the sauces. Noodles will add 164 calories and 60g of rice will add 95 calories.

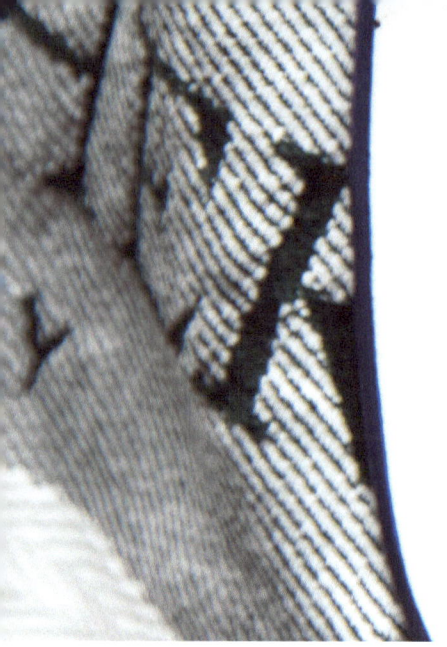

LASAGNE

This recipe was inspired by my best friend, Lana. With an Italian husband she was bound to have the best Lasagne recipe around. I may have added a twist.

SERVES: 8	KCAL/SERVE: 593	C: 37g P: 45g F: 28g

INGREDIENTS

- ½ Tbsp olive oil
- 1 brown onion - diced
- 6 cloves garlic - finely diced or crushed
- 1kg lean beef mince
- 2 tsp beef bone broth or stock powder
- 1 cup mushrooms - diced
- 1400g passata
- 1 Tbsp tomato paste
- ½ cup red wine
- 1 tsp worcestershire sauce
- 1 tsp Habanero tabasco
- fresh basil and oregano
- 50g butter
- 2 Tbsp plain flour
- 500ml full cream milk
- 300g grated colby or mozzarella cheese
- 300g fresh lasagne sheets

MAINS ◊ TREATS

METHOD

1. Heat olive oil in a pan.
   Add the onion and garlic then cook for 3 minutes.
   Add the mince and stock and cook until browned.
   Add the mushrooms and cook for 5 minutes.
   Add the passata, tomato paste, red wine and sauces.
   Add a good handful of chopped herbs and bring to the boil.
   Reduce the heat to low and simmer for 1-2 hours - stirring occasionally.

2. In a separate pot, on a medium-low heat, melt the butter.
   Add the flour and stir quickly using a whisk to create a paste.
   Start adding the milk, very slowly, while whisking as it thickens. Continue to add the milk until it's all gone. Then add half the cheese and salt and pepper.

3. Spread a little meat sauce on the bottom of a baking dish so it doesn't stick - then do 3 layers:
   1 - Lasagne sheets, 2 - Mince, 3 - More herbs, 4. 1 Tbsp of white sauce. Finish with white sauce then top with the rest of the cheese.

4. Put in a 180 degree oven for 20-30 minutes until browned on top.

5. Leave to cool for 15 minutes before slicing and serving with a side of salad.

(Tip - lasagne is great the next day heated up as it keeps its shape. Also can be frozen.)

MAINS ◊ LEAN & CLEAN

BAKED FISH AND RICE

*Inspired by a girlfriend, another easy dish that can feed a crowd.
The kids will love it if you leave out the harissa, unless spice is their thing.*

SERVES: 3	**KCAL/SERVE:** 404	**C:** 38g **P:** 26g **F:** 17g

INGREDIENTS

- 1 onion - diced
- 2 cloves garlic - finely sliced or crushed
- 1 tsp paprika
- 1 tsp turmeric
- 1 tsp cumin
- 1 tsp harissa
- 1 zucchini, diced
- 1 carrot, diced
- 200g broccoli
- 50g peas
- 250g cooked brown rice
- 15ml olive oil
- 3 tsp dijon mustard
- 300g barramundi or white fish of choice
- 1 lime

METHOD

1. Put the onion and 1 clove of garlic in a pan with the spices for 3 minutes or until fragrant.

2. Add the rest of the vegetable and stir fry until cooked. Add the rice and combine well.

3. Mix the olive oil, mustard, 1 crushed garlic clove and salt and pepper then add to the pan and combine.

4. Pop the rice mixture in a baking tray and lay the fish on top. Squeeze the lime over the fish and layer lime slices on top.

5. Cover with foil and bake in a 180 degree oven for 15 minutes.

MAINS ◊ LEAN & CLEAN

KANGAROO CHILLI

If I don't tell you that this is Chris' recipe, I'll be in trouble! A signature dish of his, it makes so many servings and is a great go to when you need a quick dinner. Kangaroo is a great source of protein and iron which is low in fat and has an immense amount of micronutrients. Readily available in Australia. If you can't get kangaroo, beef is fine as a substitute.

SERVES: 9	KCAL/SERVE: 319	C: 30g P: 34g F: 5g

INGREDIENTS

- 10ml olive oil
- 1 x brown onion, diced
- 1 x clove of garlic, finely chopped
- 1kg kangaroo mince
- 1 capsicum, diced
- 130g mushrooms, diced
- 1 x El Paso Taco Spice Mix
- 1 x El Paso Burrito Spice Mix
- 1 x El Paso Spice for Fajitas
- 2 tins of kidney beans
- 2 tins of diced tomatoes
- 400g tomato paste
- 100g chopped baby spinach

METHOD

1. Heat the olive oil in a large pan, add onion and garlic and cook until soft.

2. Add kangaroo mince and cook until brown.

3. Add capsicum and mushrooms.

4. Add the spices, tomatoes, beans, paste and spinach. Stir together then leave on a low heat for 2-3 hours. (You can also use a slow cooker overnight.)

5. Serve with a jacket potato, crusty bread or brown rice. Use in your taco bowls, or as a pasta.

Can be frozen as well.

MAINS

STEW

A variation of my Dad's stew. I've spruced it up a little but the foundations are the same. Trust me, the chutney is what makes it. If you want more heat add more tabasco! Cosy for a Winter's evening and great for the whole family.

SERVES: 5	**KCAL/SERVE:** 552	**C:** 45g **P:** 52g **F:** 7.8g

INGREDIENTS

- 1kg diced beef (rump is the best or ask your butcher for the best for a slow cooked stew)
- 1 brown onion, diced
- 4 dried bay leaves
- 2 beef stock cubes - or 4 teaspoons of beef bone broth powder
- 3 medium potato, diced
- 1 large sweet potato, diced
- 2 carrots, diced
- 60 grams fruit chutney
- 60 grams mango chutney
- 15ml worcestershire sauce
- Splash of tabasco sauce
- 2 Tbsp corn flour
- 150g frozen peas

METHOD

1. Pop beef and onion in a big pot with salt and pepper, bay leaves and stock, then cover with water and bring to the boil. Turn down and simmer for an hour and a half - keeping the water topped up so that the meat is covered.

2. Add the potatoes and carrots and simmer for another hour. (You may need to top up the water.) Then add the chutneys and sauces and simmer for another 30 minutes.

3. Mix the cornflour with a little water to make a liquid paste - slowly stir that in until the sauce thickens.

4. Add the peas and mix in.

5. Serve hot with some crusty bread. Perfect for a Winter's evening.

MAINS ◊ LEAN & CLEAN

PRAWN FRIED RICE

Another super quick and easy dish the whole family will love.

| SERVES: 3 | KCAL/SERVE: 394 | C: 55g P: 26g F: 7g |

INGREDIENTS

- 1tsp vegetable oil
- 1 brown onion
- 1 red capsicum - diced
- 100g cup mushrooms - diced
- 1 carrot - diced
- 100g baby peas
- 1 egg - beaten
- 250g cooked brown rice (cooled)
- 200g cooked prawns
- 60ml oyster sauce
- 50g light soy sauce
- 1 tsp crushed garlic
- 5ml sesame oil
- 2 spring onions

METHOD

1. Heat the vegetable oil in a wok on a high heat.

2. Pop in all the veggies and the garlic (except spring onion). Stir fry until cooked, move to the side of the wok and pour in the egg. Let it cook a little on the bottom then and then mix through the veggies.

3. Add the rice, prawns, oyster sauce and soy sauce to the wok.

4. Stir fry for 3 minutes, then take off the heat and add the sesame oil and the spring onion.

Enjoy!

MAINS ◊ LEAN & CLEAN

CAULIFLOWER TACOS

The first time I made this I was experimenting and one of Chris' mates was over. Chris was sceptical that I was making a vegetarian dish for his 6 foot 4 friend. It turned out it was a huge hit and they ate the lot. A definite crowd pleaser!

SERVES: 11	**KCAL/SERVE:** 245/taco	**C:** 22g **P:** 6.7g **F:** 13g

INGREDIENTS

- 280g cauliflower
- 15ml olive oil
- 1 onion, chopped
- 1 tsp cumin
- ½ tsp chilli powder
- 75g green lentils
- 2 Tbsp of adobo sauce (From a can of chipotle peppers.)
- juice of 1 lime
- 6 tortilla small corn wraps
- 100g avocado - smashed
- coriander
- 2 cups of vegetable stock
- 50g mayonnaise (you could use vegan mayonnaise to make this dish completely vegan)
- 2 cloves garlic
- 15g tomato paste

METHOD

1. *Cauliflower*
   Preheat the oven to 200g, break the cauliflower into florets and toss them in olive oil then season with salt and pepper. Layer the florets on a baking tray and roast for around 30 minutes.

2. *Chipotle sauce*
   Whisk together the adobo sauce, the mayonaise, lime juice and salt and pepper - set aside

3. *Lentils*
   Warm olive oil in a pot and sauté the onion and garlic with a little salt for 5 minutes. Add tomato paste, cumin and chilli powder and sauté for another minute. Add the lentils and vegetable stock and bring to the boil. Turn down to simmer and cook uncovered for about 40 minutes or until the lentils are tender. Drain the excess liquid and set aside.

4. *Assembling*
   Heat the tortillas and assemble. Line the tortilla with avocado, followed by the lentil mix, then cauliflower and sauce. Sprinkle with a generous amount of coriander.

──── MAINS ◇ LEAN & CLEAN ────

TUNA JACKET POTATOES

*A super simple dish that tastes delicious.
Yummy things don't need to be complicated.*

SERVES: 1

KCAL/SERVE: 357

C: 35g **P:** 35g **F:** 12g

INGREDIENTS

- 200g potato - (Pierced and in the microwave for 5 minutes and then in a hot oven for 10 minutes to crisp.)
- 40g Greek yoghurt
- 1 spring onion
- 1 egg, hard boiled
- 70g tin of tuna in spring water - drained
- 30g sweet corn kernels
- 10g grated cheese

METHOD

1. Mix yoghurt, spring onion, chopped egg, tuna, corn, salt and pepper all together.

2. Slice open the potato, place the cheese at the bottom and add the mixture. Serve with leafy greens.

"ONE HOT DAY DOES NOT MAKE A SUMMER *eat*

SIDES

These side dishes will always impress. Everyone loves potatoes so here are my favourite ways to serve them on the side. A lean and clean option and a treat option, both of which are delicious and moorish.

SIDES

DUCK FAT POTATOES

Need I say more. The crispiest, most indulgent roast potatoes you'll ever eat. Make more than you think because everyone will go back for more, trust me!

SERVES: 6	KCAL/SERVE: 465	C: 30g P: 2.5g F: 38g

TREATS

INGREDIENTS

- 1kg red royale potatoes
- 200g duck fat
- 2 Tbsp extra virgin olive oil
- 1 Tbsp white flour
- 4-5 cloves garlic
- fresh sage

Best prepared and left in a fridge overnight.

METHOD

1. Peel and chop the potatoes in half. Place potatoes in a pot and cover with water and boil for 10 minutes.

2. Drain the potatoes in a colander and shake around to rough up the edges.

3. Sprinkle the flour over the potatoes and season well with salt.

4. Pop the olive oil into a roasting dish and lay the potatoes in. Making sure they're nice and snug. Tip over the duck fat and cover the potatoes well. Put the squashed whole garlic cloves amongst the potatoes and season well. Cover the roasting dish and pop in the fridge overnight.

5. Turn the oven on to 200 degrees to preheat. Place in the potatoes and roast for an hour. Take out and squish with a potato masher and add lots of sage leaves amongst the potatoes. Spoon over some of the hot fat from the bottom of the roasting dish over the potatoes. Put back in the oven for a further 30 minutes until nice and crisp.

Enjoy with your Sunday roast!

––––– SIDES ◊ LEAN & CLEAN –––––

FRIES WITH A TWIST

A classic favourite. Nothing better next to a piece of fresh fish or a beautifully cooked steak.

SERVES: 2

KCAL/SERVE: 214

C: 35g **P:** 4g **F:** 7g

INGREDIENTS

- 400g of white potatoes (charisma)
- 10g cornflour
- 1 Tbsp of olive oil
- ½ tsp of paprika
- salt

METHOD

1. Chop potato into matchstick size pieces.

2. Pop into a bowl and toss with the cornflour. Then add 1 Tbsp of olive oil, ½ tsp of paprika and a good amount of salt. Mix well.

3. Spread the potato out on a baking tray lined with baking paper.

4. Place in a 200 degree oven for approx 20-25 mins until chips are brown and crunchy.

SIDES ◊ LEAN & CLEAN

SWEET POTATO FRIES

Sweet potato fries - the best twist on a classic there ever was. I love a bit of chicken salt on my sweet potato fries as well.

SERVES: 2

KCAL/SERVE: 231

C: 40g **P:** 3g **F:** 7g

INGREDIENTS

- 400g of sweet potatoes
- 10g cornflour
- 1 Tbsp of olive oil
- ½ tsp of paprika
- salt

METHOD

1. Chop sweet potato into matchstick size pieces.

2. Pop into a bowl and toss with the cornflour. Then add 1 Tbsp of olive oil, ½ tsp of paprika and a good amount of salt. Mix well.

3. Spread the potato out on a baking tray lined with baking paper. Place in a 200 degree oven for approx 20-25 mins until chips are brown and crunchy.

TREATS AND SMOOTHIES

One of my favourite parts of this book is this section. When you're on a journey to become a healthier version of you, there's nothing worse than a boring snack. Incorporating some indulgence into your life is also so important for balance. My lean & clean snacks are wholesome and delicious while not interrupting any of your goals. My treats are nostalgic, as these were what mum cooked growing up. My two smoothies are full of goodness and will have you feeling full and satisfied all at the same time. Great for that on the go breaky.

AVOCADO SMOOTHIE

If you're a smoothie fan you'll love this one. A meal in one, great for everyone and an easy way to get some good nutrients in. Pop all ingredients in a blender and enjoy!

SERVES: 1	KCAL/SERVE: 379	C: 47g P: 27g F: 12g

INGREDIENTS

- 50g avocado
- 1 frozen banana (or 100g)
- 1 tsp honey
- 1/2 zucchini
- handful spinach
- 250ml unsweetened almond milk
- 1 scoop vanilla protein powder

TREATS & SMOOTHIES

SUPER PROTEIN SMOOTHIE

My favourite, easy smoothie that tastes just like a chocolate milkshake. Try keeping this away from the kids... I bet you can't. Pop all ingredients in a blender and enjoy!

SERVES: 1	KCAL/SERVE: 324	C: 31g P: 25g F: 5g

INGREDIENTS

- 1 frozen banana (or 100g)
- 250ml unsweetened almond milk
- 1/2 zucchini
- 1 scoop chocolate protein powder
- 1tsp chia seeds

LEAN & CLEAN

TREATS & SMOOTHIES ◊ LEAN & CLEAN

BANANA BREAD

Find me someone who doesn't love banana bread, young or old.
There is nothing better with a cup of tea.

SERVES: 12	KCAL/SERVE: 200	C: 24g P: 10g F: 7.6g

INGREDIENTS

- 90g vanilla protein powder
- 50g almond meal
- 20g LSA
- 75g buckwheat flour
- 10g baking powder
- 2 tsp chia seeds
- 5 dates
- 30g walnuts - chopped coarsely
- 3 medium overripe bananas - mashed
- 3 eggs
- 2 Tbsp melted coconut oil
- 1/4 cup almond milk
- 40ml maple syrup

METHOD

1. Preheat the oven to 180 degrees and line a loaf tin with baking paper.

2. Mix all the dry ingredients together. Mix all the wet ingredients then add to the dry ingredients. Mix well.

3. Pour into a loaf tin and bake for 30 minutes. Cover with foil and bake for another 30 minutes or until a skewer comes out clean.

Enjoy by itself or with your favourite spread.

CHUNKY CHOCOLATE COOKIES

This is my Mum's recipe and she swears by a cookie that has nice big chunks of chocolate in them. Eat them while they're still warm or heat in the microwave for 10 seconds to have that gooey chocolate centre.

MAKES: 18	KCAL/SERVE: 310	C: 30g P: 3.6g F: 19g

INGREDIENTS

- 250g softened butter
- 4 Tbsp caster sugar
- 4 (large) Tbsp sweetened condensed milk
- 340g plain flour
- 2 tsp baking powder
- 2 blocks of Cadbury chocolate of your choice - milk, white, caramilk (Ohh cheeky!)

METHOD

1. Cream (beat) the butter and sugar until light.

2. Add the condensed milk and continue beating. Stir in the flour and baking powder. Add big chunks of the chocolate.

3. Make into balls and place on a baking tray lined with baking paper. Press slightly with a fork.

4. Bake at 180 degrees for 10 minutes for gooey cookies or 20 minutes for firm ones.
   (I prefer gooey goodness.)

--- TREATS & SMOOTHIES ---

PROTEIN MUESLI SLICE

These are a great snack for on the go, school lunch boxes, road trips and will keep for up to a week. I love the texture of the fruit and nuts. It's hard to stop at one!

SERVES: 15	**KCAL/SERVE:** 191	**C:** 12g **P:** 10.7g **F:** 9.8g

INGREDIENTS

- 1/2 cup sultanas
- 1/4 cup cranberries
- 1/4 cup dates
- 1/2 cup almonds
- 1/2 cup walnuts
- 1/2 cup sunflower seeds
- 1/4 cup chia seeds
- 1/4 cup shredded coconut
- 1/2 tsp cocoa
- 1/2 tsp ginger
- 60g vanilla protein powder
- 1/2 cup quinoa flakes
- 1/2 tsp cinnamon
- 2 egg whites & 1 egg
- 2 Tbsp maple syrup

METHOD

1. Preheat an oven to 180 degrees.

2. Roughly chop the fruit and nuts then mix with seeds, coconut, cocoa, ginger and protein. Mix in quinoa flakes and cinnamon.

3. Beat eggs together and stir into the mixture with the maple syrup.

4. Press into a greased baking tin (18cm x 27cm approx) and bake for 15 minutes or until it starts to brown on top.

5. Slice immediately and put on a cooling rack.

   (If you prefer a smoother texture - you can pop all dry ingredients in a food processor first.)

TREATS & SMOOTHIES ◊ LEAN & CLEAN

CHRIS' PROTEIN BALLS

A quick and easy recipe that everyone will love. Chris' Protein Balls will last for up to 2 weeks in the fridge so you can have snacks for days. Of course Chris gets the credit for this one.

SERVES: 23

KCAL/SERVE: 188

C: 18g **P:** 9g **F:** 7g

INGREDIENTS

- 55g almonds
- 20g shredded coconut
- 100g sultanas
- 90g vanilla whey protein powder
- 240g pitted dates
- 200g oats
- 300g Smooth Peanut Butter or Almond Butter

METHOD

1. Mix everything except the peanut butter in a food processor for about 45 seconds. Stir in the peanut butter and add a little water to combine.

2. Roll into balls and refrigerate for up to 2 weeks. *(Can also be frozen).*

TREATS & SMOOTHIES

NANA'S CARAMEL SLICE

I remember helping mum in the kitchen when I was a kid making this. My sister and I would eat the mixture and scoop out fingerfuls of the condensed milk as she was cooking. We would then sit in front of the oven watching it cook until we could have a slice. Then, later on, it was always a mission to try and sneak some out of the tin when she wasn't looking.

(Hint: I'd double it if I were you!)

SERVES: 18	**KCAL/SERVE:** 198	**C:** 21g **P:** 1g **F:** 12g

TREATS

INGREDIENTS

Base & Top
- 185g butter
- ½ cup sugar
- ½ tsp vanilla extract
- 1 ½ cups plain flour
- 1 Tbsp cocoa

Filling
- 60g butter
- ¼ cup sugar
- 2 Tbsp golden syrup
- ½ tin condensed milk
- 1tsp vanilla extract

METHOD - BASE & TOP

1. Cream the butter and sugar in a mixer until light in appearance, add the vanilla and dry ingredients.
2. Divide mixture in half. Press one half into the base of a baking dish & wrap the other half in cling film and freeze.

METHOD - BASE & TOP

1. Melt the butter and sugar in a pot on a medium heat. Stir in the syrup and condensed milk until creamy.
2. Pour over the base. Allow to cool.
3. Grate the frozen base portion over the top of the filling.
4. Bake in a moderate oven for 30 minutes.
5. *Enjoy with a cup of tea.*

TREATS & SMOOTHIES

APPLE AND RHUBARB CRUMBLE

I love serving this dish when we have friends or family over for a Sunday roast in Winter. It warms the soul. Then, nothing better than heating it up for breakfast the next day!

SERVES: 6	**KCAL/SERVE:** 350	**C:** 65g **P:** 3.6g **F:** 8.7g

TREATS

INGREDIENTS

Filling
- 3 Granny Smith apples
  - peeled, quartered & chopped into small chunks
- 200g rhubarb
  - sliced into 2cm pieces
- ¼ cup brown sugar
- 2 tsp cinnamon
- 1 tsp nutmeg
- 1 banana
  - sliced lengthways into 3

Top
- 2 cups of plain flour
- 150g butter
- ½ cup sugar
- 1tsp baking powder
- 1tsp cinnamon

METHOD - BASE & TOP

1. Mix the apple, rhubarb, brown sugar and spices in a bowl.

2. Place half the mixture in an oven safe dish, then layer the banana on top. Top with the rest of the apple mixture.

3. Pop the flour in a bowl and rub in the butter until it resembles fine bread crumbs. (Yup, get your hands dirty.) Add the sugar, baking powder and cinnamon.

4. Pour topping over base and flatten down. Pop into a 190 degree oven for 30 minutes or until a pale golden colour.

5. Serve with hot custard or if you're English (my husband), then ice-cream.

——— TREATS & SMOOTHIES ◊ LEAN & CLEAN ———

HEALTHY CHEESECAKE

This is such a simple treat but one that won't interrupt your progress and will let you feel satisfied and full.

SERVES: 1

KCAL/SERVE: 233

C: 32g **P:** 18g **F:** 4.8g

INGREDIENTS

- Yopro yoghurt of choice (I love strawberry or passionfruit. If you don't have Yopro where you are you can use 100g of Greek yoghurt)
- mixed berries
- 1 kiwi fruit
- 1 passionfruit
- 1 digestive biscuit

METHOD

1. Pop the yoghurt in a bowl, layer with fruit then crumble your digestive over the top. *Yummo!*

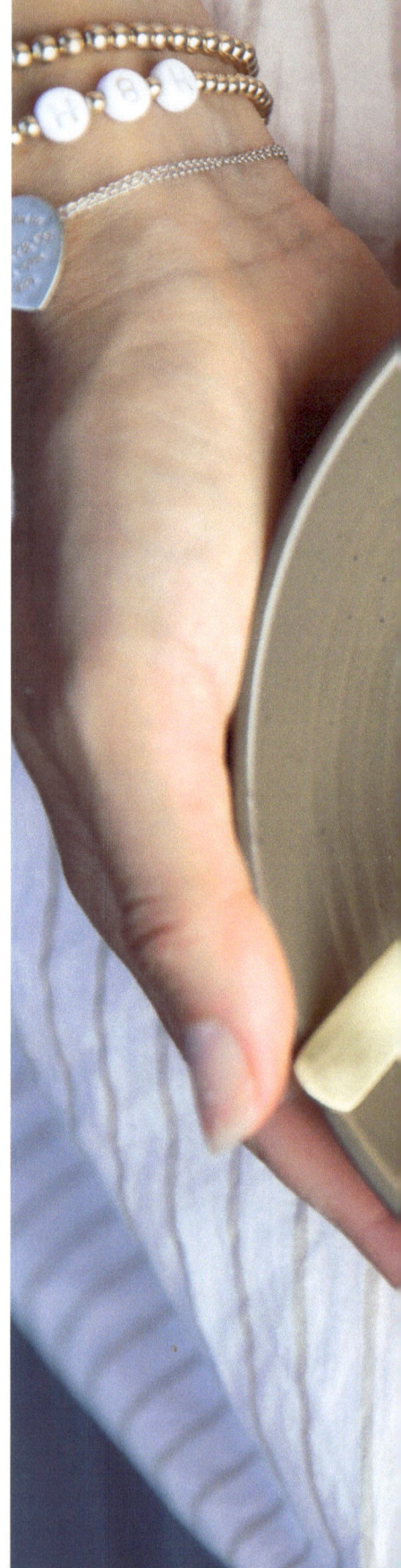

HOW TO COOK

There are loads of ways to cook these dishes - however here are my favourite, quick and easy ways to cook some basics that won't take you hours or a tonne of prep.

CHICKEN BROTH

Use it for soup, stews, as a drink or as a base for sauces and gravies.

INGREDIENTS

- 1 roast chicken carcass
- 1 carrot, diced thickly
- 2 celery sticks, diced thickly
- 1 red onion, quartered
- 3 cloves of garlic, squashed
- 3 sprigs of rosemary
- 2 cinnamon sticks
- 4 bay leaves, dried
- 3 nutmeg
- Cracked salt
- 2 tsp whole peppercorns

METHOD

1. Pop all of the ingredients into a large pot and cover with water. Bring to the boil, then reduce to a very slow simmer with the lid on and leave it.

2. You can leave this overnight - the longer the better. You need to keep topping it up with water as it reduces. You want to be left with 2 litres of beautiful chicken broth.

RICE/QUINOA

This may be a little unconventional but it works every time for me - I like quick, no thinking, easy ways to do things.

Pop the desired amount of rice or quinoa in a pot and cover with water until water sits about 2cm above the rice/quinoa. Bring to the boil then turn down the heat to low and put a lid on. Leave for approx 10 mins or until all the liquid has been absorbed. Little bubbles will form on the top when it's ready. Fuff with a fork - and voila - easy as.

SALMON

Pop salmon fillets on a baking tray lined with paper. Drizzle with a little olive oil, squeeze of lemon, crushed garlic as well as salt and pepper. Pop in a 180 degree oven for 15 minutes. Serve with pumpkin and goats cheese salad and a jacket potato.

WHITE FISH

Pop 10g of plain flour in a bowl with some salt and pepper, or your favourite seasoning. Coat the fish lightly in the flour. Heat a fry pan with 5ml of vegetable oil and pop in the fish cooking for 3-4 minutes each side. Serve with fries and some steamed greens.

CHICKEN

Coat chicken tenderloins in your favourite rub - I love a texan style smokey rub. Spray a fry pan and place in the chicken. Cook for 5 minutes each side until brown. Turn the heat down to low and spoon a tbsp of your favourite barbeque sauce over the tenderloins with 2 tbsp water. Turn continuously to coat the chicken & leave for 2 minutes until the sauce has thickened again.

POACHED PEARS

There is nothing better than poached pears on porridge, homemade granola, pancakes or even weetbix for the kids (or big kids).

Peel and quarter pears and pop in a pot. Cover with water, add 1 tsp of cinnamon (or a cinnamon stick if you have one) 1 tsp of vanilla extract or 2 tsp of essence, 2 tsp of honey. Cover with baking paper leaving a hole in the middle. Simmer on a medium to low heat for 20-25 minutes. Serve immediately or refrigerate ensuring that you store them with all the juice.

RHUBARB

If you love the pear this is pears best friend - a match made in heaven. Spoon some over your porridge, on your granola or serve with your favourite yoghurt.

Chop 500g of rhubarb into 2cm pieces. Pop in a pot with 100g sugar, 1 tsp of cinnamon and 1 tsp of vanilla extract or 2 tsp of essence. Put on a medium heat and continuously stir until most of the rhubarb has broken down and is glossy.

THANK YOU

I can't believe this has finally come to fruition! I have a few people I must thank that have helped to make this happen.

Firstly to my beautiful photographer, *Michelle,* she made every dish look so delicious and enticing and we had a ball shooting them all.

My graphic and creative designer, *Helena,* who made this book look incredible. Her attention to details and creative input were second to none and I couldn't have done this without her. Thank you for helping my dream come to life.

To my lovely editor, *Hayley,* who offered so kindly to make sure my spelling and grammar were correct.

To *Brooke,* without who I wouldn't have got this done. Thank you for helping me prep and stay organised in the lead up, whilst also looking after the twins and keeping my life in order.

Thank you to *Bethany and Kacie* for helping on the shoot and looking after babies in between.

Lastly... Thank you, *Chris,* for your patience and support as I worked tirelessly to make this happen.

xo Danni

THE AUTHOR

DANNI DUNCAN

nutrition and fitness coach

ABOUT THE AUTHOR

Danni Duncan is a qualified and featured Nutrition and Fitness coach, mum of three children Harper, and twins, Harlow and Beau, and author of Yummy - It's all about balance.

Danni loves helping women at all stages of life improve their health, mentally and physically, through exercise and balanced eating habits.

She recognised her passion for educating women after seeing the huge changes they were making through her guidance. Her online coaching programs have helped thousands of women transform themselves physically and mentally while juggling children and careers, all while not giving up the good things in life.

She is now on a mission to educate and help women all over the world be fit, healthy, happy and confident.

One of my favourite things about a hard cover recipe book is that you can scribble as much as you want it in. If I look back through my favourite recipe books there are notes everywhere - from notes about the recipe, if I should double it, anything I added or took away, or the date we had it with friends as a memory. So here's a space for all your scribble too.

FURTHER READING

Eat for Health - the Australian Dietary Guidelines
Accessed via: https://www.eatforhealth.gov.au/

Physical Activity guidelines for all Australians
https://www.health.gov.au/health-topics/physical-activity-and-exercise/physical-activity-and-exercise-guidelines-for-all-australians

INDEX

A

almond milk
  avocado smoothie 86
  banana bread 89
  overnight oats 27
  porridge 29
  super protein smoothie 87

apples
  apple and rhubarb crumble 99

avocado
  avocado smoothie 86
  cauliflower tacos 70
  pumpkin, beetroot and goats cheese salad 45
  taco bowls 56

B

bacon
  chicken and bacon carbonara 37

banana
  apple and rhubarb crumble 99
  avocado smoothie 86
  banana bread 89
  banana pancakes 23
  crepes 21
  overnight oats 27
  porridge 29
  super protein smoothie 87

basil
  lasagne 60

beans
  chicken and vegetable soup 55
  kangaroo chilli 65
  taco bowls 56

beef
  lasagne 60
  stew 67
  taco bowls 56

beetroot
  broccoli and kale salad 49
  pumpkin, beetroot and goats cheese salad 45

berries
  banana pancakes 23
  crepes 21
  granola 24
  healthy cheesecake 100
  overnight oats 27
  protein muesli slice 93

bread
  banana bread 89
  chicken and vegetable soup 55
  kangaroo chilli 65
  stew 67

broccoli
  baked fish and rice 63
  broccoli and kale salad 49
  chicken stir fry 59
  salmon and broccoli pasta 39

C

carrot
  baked fish and rice 63
  chicken and vegetable soup 55
  chicken broth 103
  chicken stir fry 59
  prawn fried rice 69
  stew 67
  taco bowls 56

cauliflower
  cauliflower tacos 70

cheese
  chicken and bacon carbonara 37
  healthy cheesecake 100
  lasagne 60
  omelette 31
  prawn and chorizo pasta with garlic and chilli 43
  pumpkin, beetrot and goats cheese salad 45
  tuna jacket potatoes 73

chicken
  chicken and bacon carbonara 37
  chicken and sundried tomato pasta 41
  chicken and vegetable soup 55
  chicken broth 103
  chicken stir fry 59
  how to cook 105

chilli
  cauliflower tacos 70
  chicken and bacon carbonara 37
  kangaroo chilli 65
  prawn and chorizo pasta with garlic and chilli 43
  taco bowls 57

chocolate
  chunky chocolate cookies 91
  overnight oats 27
  super protein smoothie 87

chorizo
  prawn and chorizo with garlic and chilli 43

coconut
  banana bread 89
  chicken and bacon carbonara 37

INDEX

chris' protein balls 95
granola 24
overnight oats 27
protein muesli slice 93

D

dates
banana bread 89
chris' protein balls 95
granola 24
protein muesli slice 93

E

egg
banana bread 89
banana pancakes 23
chicken and bacon
    carbonara 37
crepes 21
eggs 4 ways 30
prawn fried rice 69
protein muesli slice 93
tuna jacket potatoes 73

F

fish
baked fish and rice 63
how to cook 105

flour
apple and rhubarb
    crumble 99
banana bread 89
chunky chocolate
    cookies 91
crepes 21
duck fat potatoes 79
how to cook 105
lasagne 60
nana's caramel slice 97
stew 67

G

garlic
baked fish and rice 63
broccoli and kale salad 49
cauliflower tacos 70
chicken and bacon
    carbonara 37
chicken and sundried tomato pasta 41
chicken broth 103
chicken stir fry 59
duck fat potatoes 79
how to cook 104
kangaroo chilli 65
lasagne 60
prawn and chorizo pasta with
    garlic and chilli 43
prawn fried rice 69
salmon and broccoli pasta 39
taco bowls 56

goats cheese
pumpkin, beetroot and goats
    cheese salad 45

H

honey
avocado smoothie 86
chicken stir fry 59
grain salad 47
granola 24
poached pears 106
porridge 29

K

kale
broccoli and kale salad 49

L

lemon
chicken and bacon

carbonara 37
crepes 21
grain salad 47
how to cook 104
salmon and broccoli pasta 39

lentils
cauliflower tacos 70
chicken and vegetable soup 55
grain salad 47

M

maple syrup
banana bread 89
banana pancakes 23
crepes 21
granola 24
protein muesli slice 93

mushroom
chicken and bacon
    carbonara 37
chicken and sundried tomato pasta 41
chicken stir fry 59
kangaroo chilli 65
lasagne 60
omelette 31
prawn fried rice 69
taco bowls 56

N

nuts
banana bread 89
broccoli and kale salad 49
grain salad 47
granola 24
overnight oats 27
protein muesli slice 93
pumpkin, beetroot and goats
    cheese salad 45

INDEX

O

oats
banana pancakes 23
Chris' protein balls 95
granola 24
overnight oats 27
porridge 29

P

pasta
chicken and bacon carbonara 37
chicken and sundried tomato pasta 41
prawn and chorizo pasta with garlic and chilli 42
salmon and broccoli pasta 39

pears
poached pears 106

peas
baked fish and rice 63
chicken and vegetable soup 55
chicken stir fry 59
prawn fried rice 69
stew 67

potato
chicken and vegetable soup 55
duck fat potatoes 79
fries 80
stew 67
tuna jacket potatoes 73

prawns
prawn and chorizo with garlic and chilli 43
prawn fried rice 69

protein powder
avocado smoothie 86

banana bread 89
banana pancakes 23
Chris' protein balls 95
overnight oats 27
porridge 29
protein muesli slice 93
super protein smoothie 87

Q

quinoa
grain salad 47
how to cook 104
protein muesli slice 93

R

rhubarb
apple and rhubarb crumble 99
how to cook 107

rice
baked fish and rice 63
chicken stir fry 59
how to cook 104
kangaroo chilli 65
prawn fried rice 69
taco bowls 56

S

salad
broccoli and kale salad 48
grain salad 47
pumpkin, beetroot and goats cheese salad 45

salmon
grain salad 46
how to cook 104
omelette 31
salmon and broccoli pasta 39

smoothie

avocado smoothie 86
super protein smoothie 87

soup
chicken and vegetable soup 55

spinach
avocado smoothie 86
kangaroo chilli 65
omelette 31
poached eggs 30
pumpkin, beetroot and goats cheese salad 45

sweet potato
chicken and vegetable soup 55
fries 81
stew 67

T

tomatoes
broccoli and kale salad 49
cauliflower tacos 70
chicken and bacon carbonara 37
chicken and sundried tomato pasta 41
grain salad 47
kangaroo chilli 65
lasagne 60
omelette 31
prawn and chorizo pasta with garlic and chilli 43
pumpkin, beetroot and goats cheese salad 45
taco bowls 56

tuna
tuna jacket potatoes 73

www.ingramcontent.com/pod-product-compliance
Lightning Source LLC
Chambersburg PA
CBHW041412160426
42811CB00107B/1776